0

EVERY PICTURE TELLS

By

Colin Mitchell

Published by Caledonian Books LTD

First published in 2015 by Caledonian Books LTD. Edinburgh, Scotland.

www.caledonianbooks.com Printed in
the U.K
ISBN 978-0-9934532-0-5

Acknowledgement

This book may never have seen the light of day if it had not been for other people. It is only right
that I thank firstly my wife, Chris for her understanding during the writing of these
Poems and for being the catalyst that re-awakened my poetic thoughts. For not asking why I was
writing in the early hours of the morning – just simply accepting that that's what happens when
creativity strikes.

The five paintings in this book are the work of my twin sister Suzi Hiscutt and truly inspired me to
write. They are reproduced here with her kind permission.
Winter Sun at Widemouth Bay, Cornwall (Guardians)
Wheelers Bay, Isle of Wight (Marine Music)
Crashing Seas (Savage Sea)
Lamorna Cove (The Cove)
Botallack Mines, West Cornwall (Watching, Listening Tombstones)

To Chris

FOREWORD

Every Picture Tells is the teasing cliff-edge title for Colin Mitchell's first published anthology of poetry.

What Colin delivers within this slim book of around 50 or so poems explains the title: with the poetry comes illustration – paintings by Colin's very own twin sister, artist Suzi Hiscutt.

While she tells her stories through paintings Colin paints his stories in verse on the imagination. What we get is a nice serendipity of poesy and paint walking hand in hand through the book.

All the poetry content, of course, is Colin's and it's as if he had opened the floodgates of stored memories, insights and emotions.

It would not be diminishing Colin as a revealed poet to say he is now, possibly, also our resident poet. He has been with us in West Lothian for a virtual lifetime, having emigrated north from Cornwall.

His link with the south coast – and, of course, his twin – inspires him to include some vivid imagery of a wild coastline and seascape, against a background of his sister's paintings.

His poetry, does, however, range even wider, over life and times and varied topics. His is a broad canvas, as if trying to cram in all the things he's been aching to say for a long time.

Although his verses about earth and sea are to be best remembered, Colin has something to say about most things. And, as we find, Colin can surprise you. He can have a different take on things.

For example, the effrontery in taking none other than Rabbie Burns, the bard himself, to task for neglecting Bonnie Jean, leaving her at hame with the weans while he went "a wick dippin', aince or twice". "A Word in Yer Lug, Dear Rabbie" is a hoot.

And then there's "Jesus isn't just for Christmas" finger-wagging in "That Man Shall Live". And the startling missing line of a battlefield poem that leaves you teetering over a soldier's dying. But what stays best with me is the story of the bereft belfry and abandoned churchyard on East Calder's main street. This is a little gem of poetic mourning.

I have known Colin, of course, as a near neighbour, but most will know of him as a stalwart of the local amateur dramatics scene. Now he is writing his own scripts, so to speak.

By Bill Allsopp

4

Backgrounds:

CONFLICT

Having read an article concerning letters etc to and from 'The Front' one night before going to sleep, I found myself wide awake at 3am with the words of 'To the millions who gave' coursing through my mind. We always remember those who sadly died during the conflict of World War 1 but my thoughts turned more to the people left behind. What was life like for them? Hence, 'My Daddy', 'My Husband is Gone' and 'The Garden Shed' go some way to fill the picture of life away from the front line. These poems are not meant to shock, just simply to envisage how things may have been for those at home during times of conflict.

FANTASY

My time in amateur drama has opened my eyes to a world of fiction and fantasy – particularly during pantomime season – a world where the only limit to possibilities is your imagination. Inspiration for these poems comes from these stories and others of myth and magic.

HUMOUR

We all need humour to lighten our days and these aim to give a light-hearted look at the world. 'What Have You To Moan About' was the product of my mother-in-law saying that she had heard or read somewhere of the 'riches' bestowed on a woman in her later years. 'I Don't Want To Jump' on the other hand came from seeing someone trying to saddle a pony in one of the fields near me. The pony certainly wasn't up for it and I remember the scene with a smile. 'The Card Game' is a by-product of entertaining my mother-in-law and serves as a warning to those daring to challenge the elderly.
Other poems in this section cover all kinds of views on life, from innuendo to vegetables and 'The Battle Of Ward 14' is still displayed on the Red Dot Radio studio wall.

NATURE

The wonders of nature never fail to astound me and this section is devoted to the wonderful sights and sounds that surround us. From the sea and the sound of birds to the magnificence of sunrises and sunsets, I feel honoured to be present at these times and inspired by the artwork of my twin sister Suzi Hiscutt.

REFLECTIVE

Profound thoughts of things gone by and memories provide the background to many facets of life. From the sad times to the comedic capers of children – all things are character building and are not forgotten. Empathy and imagination also play their parts here and leave us with pondering thoughts of others.

RELIGION

Religion is a difficult topic with so many stories available. This is not and will never be to everyone's liking but simply a collection of my thoughts from the Christian stories I've heard and read.

SCOTS

I have lived the majority of my life in Scotland and have become accustomed to the language and dialect. As there is no-one who comes close to the works of one Robert (Rabbie) Burns with regard to the quantity and quality of poetry in this country, I took a look at his other side and the last poem in this book is my attempt to have 'A Word In Yer Lug, Dear Rabbie' as possibly spoken by a friend in an Edinburgh bar.

CONTENTS

CONTENTS

TO THE MILLIONS WHO GAVE

We can never imagine
While we live our lives so free,
The hell that you all went through
For the sake of people like me;
The memories you found there
The happy and the sad
That live with you for ever
Whether for good or bad.

Volunteers from round the world
The Commonwealth as well
But bullets care not where you're from
They just made sure you fell
Beside your friends and colleagues
Who didn't even have the time
To mourne another's passing
Cut down in his prime.

The letters home describing
Trench warfare at its worst
Each second – just wondering
Where the next deadly shell would burst.
Rain and mud and endless hours
Trying to keep dry;
Not really understanding
And always wondering why?

You never know the enemy
And the ignorance is bliss;
It's just someone you have to kill
Before *you're* blown to bits –
Except on Christmas Day that is
When all hostilities cease
And everyone relaxed for once
In a strange and alien peace.

The families waiting there at home
Who prayed for this to end;
Begging that the Lord above
His peace to loved ones send
The hope that men would soon return
But telegrams come again
Another life is over;
Their prayers are all in vain.

On and on for many years
The battles at 'The Front'
Soldiers bravely find the will
Knowing they will take the brunt
Of all the enemy gives them
Shrapnel, bullets and bombs
The knee deep quagmire soon becomes
More sappers' morbid tombs.

The heartbreak suffered back at home
Does nothing to dispel
The truly gut-wrenching horror
Of the trenches' living hell.
So many troops on either side
Would never be seen again;
This 'War to end all wars' would be
The end for so many men.

We cannot ever imagine
The 'sense' behind such deeds,
Just remember the freedom that we have
Was forged in our hour of need.
May all the lost souls find peace at last
And may we always remember
The sacrifice laid down for us,
Each and every November.

MY DADDY

"My Daddy's not home today," I say
To the man standing at the door
"I don't know when I'll see him
He's gone away to war."

My Mummy comes up behind me
To speak with this strange man;
He gives to her a letter;
She gently takes my hand.

We go into the kitchen;
She seems to be upset;
I ask her "What's wrong Mummy?"
She says she can't say yet.

She opens up the letter
As her eyes fill up with tears;
But why won't she just tell me?
A sob is all I hear.

Then she screams, so loudly
And throws the letter away;
"Oh God!", she yells at the window,
This isn't a very good day!

I'd like to play with David next door
But I don't think it very wise
To ask her now 'cos she's angry;
She just sits down and cries.

I just go over and hug her
And hope the tears will stop;
She holds me very tightly
And allows her eyes to drop.

A tear lands on my face as I
Gaze up at her and grin,
I feel it running down my cheek
And hanging off my chin.

I don't know why she's crying;
I didn't do anything bad;
Is it the man who came to the door
Who's made her feel so sad?

Then it stops, she takes a breath
And squeezes me again,
"I've something to tell you angel"
Her face is one of pain.

"You know your Daddy went away
To help out in the war?
Well, that man came with a letter
We won't be as before."

"Daddy was in a battle, you see
But now he's gone to Heaven."
I don't understand, this is so hard
'Cos I am only seven.

"You mean he won't be coming home?"
I ask with a tear in my eye;
"No, he won't." is all she says,
It's now my turn to cry.

The games we played in the garden,
The fun we had, him and me –
They've now all gone for ever;
Why does this have to be?

MY HUSBAND IS GONE

My husband is gone to fight in the war
Like so many more from this town;
There's hardly a man to be seen here
But we won't let that get us down.

The weeks pass slowly and children ask
When will Daddy be back?
I cannot answer for I do not know
When I will see my man, Jack.

A letter arrived - he's over in France
Doing his bit for the war;
He's met some new friends but wishes
He'd see himself at our door.

Weeks into months and Christmas is near,
I miss him so dreadfully;
I sent him a parcel of things from the kids
And a lock of hair from me.

I get scared in the night as I lie awake
Thinking of him over there
And wondering if he misses me as much
And will he really take care.

He's coming home! I can hardly believe
He's getting some leave from it all;
The kids are so happy and I am just thrilled,
Seems God has answered my call.

The town's getting ready, our boys will be here
The day after tomorrow they say;
There's bunting and signs all over the street
My Jack is on his way.

And then in the morning with one day to go
I hear a knock at the door;
A telegram is in my hand –
My heart's been smashed by the war.

My Jack won't be marching tomorrow;
He won't see the kids and me;
He won't be coming home again;
His face I'll never see.

My husband is gone; he fought in the war;
Nothing more can I say;
Our world is shattered, the kids and me
Now that Jack has gone away.

SEARCHLIGHTS

A howling warning shatters peace again –
Enemy planes cause death and suffering;
Explosions heard and smoke clouds towering
Above a city full of angst and pain.
This destruction that we suffer is insane;
Yet here's a glimmer of our hopes held high –
Pale beams streak across a jet black sky,
A searchlight finds the source of killing rain;
A raider lit from 'neath, this hell below,
The target for defense, our guns to bear;
This demon in the sky – he does not care
And changes life down here to one of woe.
Return to lands from whence you bloody came!
And leave us here to care for all our maimed!

Defending guns with voices yet unheard
Above the din of falling bombs and bricks,
Reducing someone's home to charcoaled sticks,
Smothering ground where bodies lie interred.
Guns tracking path of searchlight leading high
Latch onto target flying deadly, still;
The massive ROAR as shells seek out to kill
Before another soul down here's to die;
Fire forth once more – a hit! A bloody hit!
No searchlight needed now, the sky ablaze
Still seen above this penetrating haze
As downwards plummets victim, brightly lit.
But they are also all some mothers' sons –
So, after this, are we the guilty ones?

THE BATTLEFIELD

The thunderous crash is all around
As we face another day;
Things exploding everywhere,
My best mate blown away.

This carnage of the battlefield
Is wearing us all down
And just to gain a hundred yards
To a tiny little town!

Another boom and shrapnel flies
Ripping the air asunder;
Aaagh! My arm! Oh God it hurts!
Amid this dreadful thunder.

They are getting closer now
And we, at the end, are caught
In a hellish inescapable trap;
For everything, we've fought.

Somebody lands beside me;
John! Is that really you?
No answer comes, I look again
At a body broken in two.

Oh Jesus when will this all end?
"I've had enough!" I scream;
Someone wake me from this hell
And tell me it's a dream.

To all those folk I know at home
And the things I've seen and done,
My thoughts now turn and linger
For sure my end is come.

Remember me my love, my boys
As you saw me last we met;
You'll never see me home again
But I'll be with you yet.

There's no escape, Lord take me now,
The pain's more than I can stand;
My ears are ringing, my body throbs,
Can't see my bloody hand!

I'm on my back! What happened then?
My screams are all I hear
And suddenly, I know I'm done

THE GARDEN SHED

The garden shed is overgrown
Your haven lies untouched
Can't bring myself to go there
I miss you far too much

The war has taken you from me
My world's an empty shell
This loneliness and deep despair
Are driving me through hell

Three years ago today it came
That dreadful telegram
It's taken everything I had
I don't know who I am.

The tears still flow after all these years
I see you in your shed
But it's only wishful thinking
You're only in my head.

Am I really being selfish?
There's others just like me
Who've lost their dearest loved ones
Whose minds will ne'er be free.

It hurts so much to be here
Don't think I can go on
I want to be beside you
How can that be wrong?

But you are now in Heaven
And I must stay right here
One day we'll be together
Please wait for me my dear.

The garden shed is overgrown
A shrine, it stands for you
A part of you that's with me
The rest of my life through.

THOUGHTS OF A FAIRY-TALE PRINCESS

Alone and trapped here in this tower
I've lived a hundred years –
Tens of thousands of sleepless nights;
No company but my tears.

A wicked fairy put me here
And left me to myself;
While time stands still around me
I'm still here on the shelf!

Only a Prince's kiss can save
Me from this tower of doom;
Oh Knight! Please hear my cry, come forth
To find me in this room.

What's that? A mighty trumpet blare?
Can my saviour be nigh?
I rush to gaze on fields below
And pray he will not die

As many others did before –
Too many now to count;
All came this way to save me here,
Each on a sturdy mount.

I see him in the distance now,
But he is not alone!
Can this be really happening?
How could he not have known?

The curse that witch did on me cast
States clearly he must be
Unaccompanied by mortal soul
If he's to set me free!

He's reached the forest that surrounds
This prison I am in;
The trees and briars part like waves
My hopes I on him pin.

But who the hell's this other guy?
He'll ruin this, I'm sure –
The forest's melting clean away
They'll soon be at the door!

Oh how can they be so stupid?
They're beaten – like the rest;
Is there no man can see the way
To win this dire quest?

I'm getting really angry now,
This simply isn't fair;
Building my hopes on such as him
Drives me into despair.

I hear his voice shout from below
Something about my hair;
Calls out a name – Rapunzel?
What *is* wrong with this pair?

"That's not my name!" I shout to them;
A silence falls around,
"Then who the hell are we to save?
A Princess, I'll be bound."

They're from another Fairy-tale!
Of that, I am quite sure
But beggars can't be choosers now –
They're standing at the door.

A mighty crash as it falls in
Thanks to my hero's sword;
He'll soon be at the topmost stair,
My master and my lord.

A sound I hear behind me too
But I must fear the worst –
The evil witch has just returned;
Again my rescue's cursed!

"I said that he must come alone!"
She cackled in my face
A voice comes from the window now,
"We'll put you in your place!"

"No mortal I", he then declared,
"But a powerful Fairy King!"
Casting a spell as round the room
He flew on gossamer wing.

The witch, defeated, fled the scene
And to his arms I ran
"I'd go with him", I thought myself,
"Forget the other man!"

But Fairy-tales don't end this way ☹
The Prince would have to do
And though he's really second best
I'll learn to love him too.

So from the evil place we fled
As if our mount had wings;
Off to a land of happy folk
And only pleasant things.

Friends, take heed of my story
For in the hours of doubt,
When you are at your lowest ebb
Someone will help you out.

IN FAIRYLAND

Behold, we are the creatures of the night
Who live in peace in dark and shaded glen
Far from the sight of ordinary men
Who see us as such beasts of dreadful fright
Yet know not what it is that forms our plight
For blind are they to things beyond their ken
And so in peace we live our lives and then
Work magic under moon, now at its height
We fairies and such creatures busy are
As wings a-flutter fill the night with sound –
For nature keeps us all to duty bound –
To tend the living plants both near and far;
And tiny dragons are our company –
On shoulder, keeping watch that we be free.

LE PERE FOUETTARD

Le Père Fouettard (French for *The whipping Father*) was a character who went with St. Nicholas in his rounds at Christmas giving the naughty children the whip while St. Nick gives gifts to the well behaved. He wore a long, dirty, dark coloured robe and had a beard that was poorly groomed.
He is known mainly in the Eastern regions of France. In Alsace, Le Père Fouettard is synonymous with the bogeyman.

Rejoice! Rejoice! For Santa comes this way!
See all good children, each face full of joy;
But who's walking with him? Man or a boy?
A shabby dark being whose name none say
He's an evil man, beard full of decay
Looks for the child heathen who acts so coy
Whose mischief doth break another child's toy
For them this is not a very nice day
"Hide! Hide!" is the cry, they must not be seen
By Le Père Fouettard with whip in his hand
He'll thrash every one of them and demand
That they change their ways from what they have been
Punishment meted, the bully once more
Runs away frightened and closes the door.

MISCHIEF (Of a Leprechaun)

You do not know who 'tis in shadows deep,
Who ventured into daylight on this day
And murdered this poor soul to let decay
Enfold this Fairy where she lies asleep.
For on St Patrick's Day she came to me;
Such pretty wings and gown of em'rald green,
Her face had not by any man been seen;
She said, "For you my heart will ever be."
Her vile intention was to slowly woo
My heart and all the things I hold so dear;
A hand I raised, with my intention clear –
I threw a spell and clove her frame in two.
I stand accused! Her love I could not touch –
A Leprechaun can never love that much!

THE 'BEAST' OF BODMIN MOOR

'tis night and shapes of rock and tree
Change in imagination
As mist and fog roll ever on
Fill land with trepidation

For what's unseen and only heard
Feeds man's thoughts unbound
Plays tricks on senses heightened here
Brings threat to every sound

Deathly mist begins to fall
Its journey at an end
But whence it came nobody knows
Through flesh its shivers send

'tis thicker now than e'er before
And shrouded in its fold
Man feels the icy, sodden touch
Turn heart and limbs to cold

A numbness sets the mind away
On journey dark and fraught
Imagination fills the brain
With terrifying thought

A sound rides in on wafted wind
An eerie, chilling moan
Is there black magic in its voice
Which finds man all alone?

A dev'lish sound, it rises high
And fills the air of night
But senses cannot track it down
Thoughts turn to headlong flight

But into what? The mist's so thick
That nothing here be seen
And marrow's chilled to freezing point
A man can only scream

This hellish place, now peril-filled
Appears to be the last
That man will see upon this Earth
Where he will breathe his last

Another sound! A cracking twig
Spins man around alarmed
And dreadful things fill every thought
The mind already harmed

Witches, warlocks, beasts and all
The evil of this place
Now enter into fearful sense
Heart hammers at a pace

Streaming tears fall ever down
His visage panic-stricken
Does he by fate or destiny
Fall foul of local Wiccan?

Then moan returns to haunt again
And pierces racing mind
There's no way out of living hell
There's no escape to find

Darker, damper, colder now
Sounds heighten to a roar
A growl so fierce seems everywhere
Chills man to very core

The shriek of swooping feathered fiend
A rustle to the left
Finds man fall flat upon the ground
Of common sense bereft

A silent prayer, unheard by all
Escapes such trembling lips
As evil ever-closer comes
He into darkness slips.

WHAT HAVE YOU TO MOAN ABOUT?

An old man listened to them moaning
About a woman's woes;
Then rose to his feet and told them
Of how a woman's day goes.

You've nothing at all to moan about
You women gathered here –
You've more today than you ever had,
You've nothing at all to fear!

There's riches untold with you every day;
Like the SILVER in your hair –
Just ponder on the memories
Of those who put it there.

You've a fortune lying inside your mouth
With copious fillings of GOLD,
So don't be saying you've nothing
With a mouthful of riches untold.

There are CRYSTALS in your kidneys
And STONES in your bladder too;
You're worth an enormous fortune
Is all I say to you.

It's true you may walk slowly
As you amble down the street,
But that is all because you have
So much LEAD in your feet

When the vicar suggests the 'hereafter'
Is worth a thought or two,
You remind him that you've done that –
It's part of your life too.

Be it in the upstairs bedroom
Or at the kitchen sink;
No matter where you find yourself,
"What am I here after?" you think.

And as for those without a man?
Don't talk such nonsense now,
You've more men than you really know –
Please let me tell you how.

When you wake up in the morning
WILL POWER's at your side;
He gets your feet out on the floor
And tells you not to bide.

A toddle to the bathroom's next –
A visit to your JOHN,
And once your ablutions are finished
It's time to soldier on.

The next fellow to come calling
Is an ever-lasting guy –
ARTHUR RITIS joins you next
And doesn't say goodbye.

He's with you all the long day through
And keeps you company
By moving round from joint to joint;
From him you're never free.

You flirt with another gentleman,
AL ZHEIMER or what's his name?
You never can remember,
To you it's all the same.

Your good friend JOHNNY WALKER comes
To keep your spirits high
And brings along JACK DANIELS
Until the evening's nigh.

The time just flies with all these men
And so after such a day
You head, once more, to the bedroom
With your good friend EARL GREY.

So don't regale all your moans and woes,
You've a life that's really fine;
Such treasures and male company –
I wish that life was mine

But in my dotage, I have to say
There's just one friend for me;
She wakes me in the wee small hours
Her name? ANITA P

I DON'T WANT TO JUMP

I don't want to jump those fences;
I don't want to run, do you hear?
I don't want to jump those fences
My eyes are wide with fear!

I don't care if it's the Grand National!
I don't want to jump, understand?
I don't want to jump those fences
Don't rub my neck with your hand!

It's no use cajoling or urging;
You'll be sorry you started this –
I don't want to jump those fences
It's always a hit or a miss.

The others look calm, but inside
I'm panicking like hell;
I don't want to jump those fences
Or run at the sound of that bell.

I don't want to jump those fences
The tape is raised, they're off!
But I don't want to jump those fences;
I think I'm getting a cough.

I don't want to jump those fences
My hooves will get all marked;
I don't want to jump those fences
I'm really getting quite narked!

I'm running, I don't know what happened,
The first fence is coming up fast;
I don't want to jump those fences
But I don't want to be last

I don't want to jump those fences
But here it comes, Oh God!
The others leap and I must too;
This jockey's a crazy sod!

I told you I didn't want to jump
But you wouldn't listen to me
So now you sit there on the grass
And I am running freeee!

THE CARD GAME

Joined a game of cards today
Thought, "This'll be a lark!"
Against an octogenarian
With a mind so evil and dark

She claimed to not know what she did
But out of the hands we played
My attempts to win a single trick
Were stamped out or delayed.

The schemes she used to win each hand
Were things I'd never seen –
'Mistakenly' playing a nine or six
And claiming "It's a Queen"!

Her failing sight was blamed for this
And her hearing wasn't great
So finally I won a trick,
Beating her five with an eight.

A grin of smugness on my face
As she dealt the final hand,
I had the shout, how could I lose?
I was in the Promised Land.

Just one card each – I had a King!
I simply had to play it,
Excitement coursing through my veins,
Could I bring myself to say it?

"TAKE THAT!" I yelled and threw it down,
It glowed there on the table;
She looked at it and at her hand
Then with all that she was able.

Flung the flaming ACE on top
Of my poor beaten King!
I've never been so deflated,
Just couldn't believe this thing.

So please take heed, my erstwhile friend
If challenged to a game
Of anything by the elderly;
Just run and save your name.

These ancient folk are a breed apart,
Will win at any cost
And leave you in a quivering heap
Just wondering how you lost!

OO-ER MISSUS!

She held it firmly in her hand,
Unsheathed it very slowly –
Then grabbed another, did the same;
The sight was quite unholy.

She licked her lips, just couldn't wait
As to her mouth it lifted;
And teasing took the very tip
Between her teeth – so gifted!

That's not enough, I must have more!
Her thoughts were running wild
To find what else would be just right –
'twas in her memory filed.

Searching, searching till at last
Something makes her smile;
Aha! I like that little thought,
Haven't done that for a while.

Happy now, her mind drifts off
Like thought of inner-man;
Oh yes! That's it! Just like before –
Add a touch of cinnamon!

For just a sprinkling is enough
To titillate the tongue,
And you will know just when to stop –
When your spiced banana's done!

THE HAPPY RUNNER BEAN
(To the tune "Mary Anne")

A Runner bean am I, so tall;
Tied to a net so I don't fall,
Prettiest flowers of red and white;
Long green pods filled with delight.

Chorus:
I spent my time a-growin'
I spent my time a-growin'
I spent my time a-growin'
And then they cut me down!

Happy days in glorious sun,
Growing till my days are done;
Picked and sliced, this is my lot
Boiled in a metal pot!

Chorus:
I spent my time a-growin'
I spent my time a-growin'
I spent my time a-growin'
And then they cut me down!

THE PREACHER AND THE PADRE
(Warning: this poem contains profanity)

A preacher and a padre
Were on the opening green
The padre sank his putt with ease
Preacher gave his ball a clean

Replaced it on the very spot
And through gritted teeth he hissed
"Get in the goddam hole, you sh*t!"
"Damn it! Bloody missed!"

The padre taken aback by this
A word to his friend did say
"Almighty God will punish you
Upon this very day

A lightning bolt He'll send this way
And strike you where you stand
You have to stop profanities
From getting out of hand!"

The next green was the same again
The preacher, his ball kissed
The ball just edged the cup and stopped
"Damn it! Bloody missed!"

The padre mentioned once again
The wrath of God would come
If the preacher failed to mend his ways
And curb his evil tongue

Then standing on the final green
The preacher glanced the cup
With a worried look upon his face
He dared to then look up

The lightning struck the padre dead
The preacher shook his fist
A voice boomed out from up above
"Damn it! Bloody missed!"

THE BATTLE OF WARD 14

Hospital radio is a lifeline to so many people during their time in hospital. This particular station had a request programme from 8:00pm till 10:00pm. Apart from playing requests, the respective presenters would ask general knowledge questions and any patient providing the correct answer could win a pack of biscuits. The following is the tale of one particular evening...

'Twas a Monday night, the ninth of May
When battle lines were drawn
There were five of the women but only three men
And at eight they sounded the horn.

The brains were all buzzing as trivia was dredged
From the deepest parts of the mind,
An infinite mass of knowledge from the men
Better you'd be hard pushed to find.

The poor humble jocks on the Radio Show
Didn't know what was coming their way
But the battle began as soon as one man
Answered the first question right away.

The name of the maiden Perseus dragged from the sea?
"It's Andromeda!" Colin shouted out loud
So Alistair rang the radio show
"One nil to the boys!" screamed the crowd.

But what happened next took the jocks by surprise
As they started the next question that night
"Which amendment in the American constitution...."
He cut short as he had quite a fright

The telephone rang before he was done
And again the boys were quite right
When Colin called in with the answer this time
"The fifth!" was his cry in the fight.

Two-nil to the boys and they were looking strong
As the next question came over the air
'Twas about Dr Who – and historical too
But Kenny had the answer right there.

"Which of the following comedians
Never appeared on the show?
Ken Dodd, John Cleese, Harry Enfield,
Alexei Sayle", he wanted to know.

Well Kenny set his mind a-racing
On his efforts the next point was hung
He figured it out, in a method round about
Harry Enfield would be too young.

He called up the show to put forward his case
And delighted was he when he scored.
Three-nil to the boys, this is easy they thought
In danger of getting too bored.

The battle raged fiercely for minutes on end
When "Where in the world?" was asked
The first clue was given about Delft potter-y
From the seventeenth century – past.

Well Colin, being older than Ali and Ken
(Put together it seemed to some),
Checked in his history 'mind-bank' again
But the answer still wouldn't come.

They puzzled and puzzled for what seemed an age
Then Colin called out for the phone
"In 1650 they moved over to Bristol",
He was wrong – and gave a short moan.

"I'll give you the next clue," the Quiz Master said
And mentioned the "Lotter-y"
'Twas the first Grand National winner!" Colin said
"You're standing at Aint-e-ree!"

Well that earned the boys two packets – and more
A chocolate orange as well
But the girls got in with the next one that night
And shattered the winning spell.

The next was a musical question
The theme tune of a 70s show
The boys had to think – were they over the brink
Would they have to let this one go?

Not on your Nellie! "The Persuaders" Ali said,
But the Quiz Master added a catch.
He put in four bonus questions, the bam,
So another plan had to be hatched.

The boys did their best and Ali called in
But his face turned puce with rage
"The line is engaged!" he screamed in dismay
And paced like a bear in a cage.

'Twas Jean for the girls and answers she had
To gain all five points was her goal
To the boys' utter dismay the Quiz Master did say
"Five points – you're out of the hole!"

The scores were now level and tension was high
As the next question was read
"Which shipping forecast area's between
The Baillie and Shannan?" he said.

Again the boys thought, deeper than ever before
The seas around Britain to find.
There was Dogger, the Bight and Faroes as well
But Kenny had the answer in mind.

He grabbed for the phone and called back in again
The boys were back in the hunt.
The answer was Rockall and Kenny had scored
And put the boys' noses in front.

Six-five was the score but the Quiz Master had
A difficult question in store
Another theme tune to a 70s show –
The boys' brains now getting sore.

They wracked and wracked their tired brains
The answer just wasn't there
Kenny called in with some answers fine
But he was only blowing hot air.

This was the question that seemed to stump all
The boys and the women as well
No matter how much they searched their minds
They were living through some kind of hell.
Another special the Quiz Master gave
A compilation of themes,
Intro's to TV shows he played,
The brains began to teem.

They concentrated harder still
The answers were there somewhere
The girls rang in with two of them
Kenny jumped up in the air.

"They're winning!" he cried, his voice full of fear
"Get thinking! We've got to win!"
They thought they had four – so Kenny phoned up
But a blow he felt on his chin.

26

Only one of the four was right, he was told,
Was all to be lost so late?
'Twas fast approaching ten of the clock
And they had battled since eight!

At two minutes to ten the answers were aired
And the girls were awarded their two,
The boys were defeated by seven to six
So much given by so few.

Thus ended the battle of wits in fourteen
And prizes were duly brought round
A total of six small packets of bics
And a teddy were for the girls bound.

The boys got their five and a chocolate orange too,
Stood tall after such a long fight
But ladies be warned, they're not finished yet
Be ready for another tonight!!!

URBAN HUNTERS

It's sad to think the place we lived
Has now been pulled apart
We're forced onto these busy roads
Enough to break your heart

Hush now my lad, can you not see
The Sun is going down?
It's the hour for us to step outside
And then we hit the town!

Stay close by me and let me show
As we from the shadows creep
That this is such a pleasure ground
With something on every street

We'll get some food first – set us up
For the frolic we shall see
And I know a great wee watering hole
Just for you and me

So, what to have – there's such a choice
Fish suppers, Indian or
There's a Chinese round the corner
We couldn't want for more

I know there's people and it's light
But not where we are going
Just follow me around the back
Without bright lights a-glowing

A gap there is – just by the gate
That leads to joys untold
What others throw away you'll see
Is treasure for the bold

For that is what we are my boy
Bold as brass and clever
While others starve until they die
We'll be around for ever

But keep your guard about you boy
Some things can hurt you see
So stick with me and you'll be safe
And stay forever free

But trust your Dad, I'll find somewhere
For you to lay your head
It may be rather simple though
Not quite a feather bed

You see that box? Just over there?
It holds delights for us
I've seen it all before you know
Dive in! Don't make a fuss

Once we've finished we'll slip away
To another place I've been
But keep your wits about you now
By others don't be seen

I know it's not the life you want
To roam the streets at night
But things have changed for us you see
And this is now our plight

You see my boy, this" Urban" thing
Is now our forest patch
And we must just enjoy the thrills
As cunning plans we hatch

For humans stole the home we had
And those of others too
Just so they could have a house
There's nothing we can do

We'll have to live from day to day
On whatever we can find
And take it back to where we hide
Out of sight and mind

But while we live and plot and scheme
We'll give them such a fright
By making all the noise we can
In the middle of the night

For though we can't live as we did
Our ground invaded so
They'll always wonder if we are
Still here, but never know

BIRDSONG

The raucous call of the Magpie
Echoes all around;
The plaintive screech of Blackbird –
A panic-stricken sound,
Gentle twittering Blue-tit
Searching 'mongst the trees;
The beautiful song of Robin –
My ears are filled with these.

Soft cooing of the Pigeon
In the treetop tall;
The chirping of a Sparrow
Sends forth a mating call;
The tiny screech of Swallow
Streaking 'cross the sky –
A magical musical interlude
Delights both you and I.

THE SNOWFLAKE

Just consider the snowflake;
Take a moment of your time
To see the exquisite beauty;
It really is a crime
That such a fragile pretty thing,
When joined with all its brothers,
Can cause such havoc and despair
To humans and to others.

Layer upon pristine layer,
Thick upon the ground;
Covering just everything,
Falls without a sound.
So just take time to imagine,
When shovelling clear the path,
The millions of tiny snowflakes
You're killing with your wrath.

GREEN

What is this life of colour now devoid?
All dull and dreary black and white to see –
Not such a world for likes of you or me,
Naught for us there to take on Polaroid;
So Mother Nature gives so freely here
Such beauty and delight for all the world,
Shows off the wonders of her gown – unfurled
Lest through a pressing monochrome we peer;
So harken now to what I have to say –
Enjoy the colours all around us now;
The reds and blues and yellows take their bow
Upon this stage where they perform their play;
But over all of them we must have seen
That most predominant of colours – green!

For this is Mother Nature at her best;
When others have such limits on them placed,
To green She turns and fills this dreary waste
In myriad of tones to give us rest;
From palest pale to Her most vibrant hue,
She clothes the earth with subtle ling'ring shades
And cloaks of green now light the woodland glades
In such a way not many colours do;
For green She tells us is the sign of life,
When Spring comes round to end the Winter's dark
And shoots begin to form beneath the bark
To bring an end to February strife;
I honour which of Nature is the Queen
That most predominant of colours – green.

THE GULL

Proudly aloof on single leg
I stand in sun and bask;
Just biding time until I hear
The opening of a flask.

For then I know it's picnic time
On beaches down below –
Away I swoop to find a bite,
These humans! They don't know!

For I am king of the scavengers,
I take whate'er I want –
Sandwiches, pies or burgers fine
No need for me to hunt.

Not while there are such pickings here
Amongst these tourist bands;
I rake the litter bins as well
And steal from children's hands.

But just for now, I'll stand at peace –
My gorging time is done;
I'll close my eyes, well, maybe one
And snooze in summer sun.

GUARDIANS

Like battleships we stand and wait
In this war against the sea;
We are protectors of the land
And thus we'll ever be.

Craggy, cratered, crusty old men
Stand proud 'gainst mighty storm,
Break down the onward rushing wave
And never change our form.

As guardians of our sleepy bay
We stand 'twixt sea and sand;
If not for us, the crashing wave
Would swamp the humans' land.

But we are home to life as well;
Give shallow refuge here
Amongst our wrinkled faces hard
For some who live in fear.

MARINE MUSIC

How good it is to hear the gentle sound
Of sea wave coursing through the shingled shore –
This music in my ears rings evermore,
Till lost am I and in a new world found.
Soft dripping from the roof of darkest cave,
(Which sea had entered and has now recoiled)
Its walls in witness to a battle foiled,
Comes new percussion from the now-spent wave.
A breeze exudes from myriad glistening stones
To fill the background here amidst the swell
As back to shore the sea seeks out this cell
Creates such music – and in subtle tones.
No wonder then in cave and such as this
Cathedral echoes sea's orchestral bliss.

WATCHING, LISTENING TOMBSTONES

No sound of busy industry;
No men's voices down below;
Like giant tombstones, standing there
To the life we used to know.

The only sound above the surf,
The gulls' ear-piercing cry;
As if they are still mourning
The life of days gone by.

Yet even now, on gale-strewn night
Listen carefully to the sound
Of miners' voices singing;
Like angels underground.

The rhythmic rising, falling;
Wind-torn, mounting whine;
From whisper to crescendo
Sends shivers down my spine.

And when it's passed, the daylight shows
These sentinels still there;
Still watching silently o'er the cove,
Strong, resolute Cornish pair!

FOUR YEARS ON

Standing, staring, unbelieving
At what I see before me
The beauty of the Garden City
Brought almost to its knees

But more than the sight
It's the sound I hear
Or really, that I don't
As if breath is held in fear

For after all the jackhammers
Have stopped their noise for the day
Only silence lives round the Cathedral
Even birds have flown away

It once stood for peace and the love that is God
But why would He have done this?
To bring us together as we used to be
And show that we are indeed His?

A lot of this beautiful city
Has been ruined and forever is gone
But Cantabrians all will always stand tall
And show that they can be strong

Christchurch will rise again from the ash
To the credit of all those who care
For this beautiful Garden City
And the heroes with courage so rare

No, we will never forget them
The one-eighty-five lost souls
We'll pray that God now attends them
As, for them, we achieve our goals.

LONG LIVE CHRISTCHURCH

A MOTHER'S TEARS

The pain of hellish labour
Disappears the moment you
Take hold of that tiny infant
And shed a tear or two'

Those tears remain throughout their lives
Some sad and some with joy
As you nurture these tiny babes
Into toddling little boys.

Anxiety when they were ill
And worry when they cried;
So many things make memories,
With you their only guide.

Time flashes by so quickly;
Soon they're off to school;
The house is empty during the day,
Your eyes are filled like pools.

You spend your life to do the best
For them, that's all you can;
And before you really know it
Your boy's become a man.

One's headed off to Uni
Some other skills to learn;
There's exams he's still to pass if he
A living is to earn.

Then Uni's done and fear returns
That he'll be leaving home;
You've dreaded this for all these years
And now the time is come.

"I've got a house!" he smiles one day
And then it really hits;
This parenting is hard as hell,
The pain on your heart sits.

The other boy is still at home
And working every day,
So some normality remains;
He'll never go away.

You worry even more now as
Your boys have lives their own;
You still remember the little ones
Who into men have grown.

It's hard to take it on the day
The second one declares
He's thinking of adventure;
Although he knows not where.

His mind made up, he says to you
He's going to emigrate!
Excitement doesn't let him hear
Your heart begin to break.

The first son's moved to another town
And this one's going away
To the other side of the bloody world!
This is your life's worst day.

You have to hide the heartache
And just be thrilled for him;
But he will be so far away,
Your future's looking grim.

Your heart is being torn apart,
The day is getting near;
Your partner doesn't understand,
He doesn't shed a tear.

The train pulls in, quick hugs all round,
Then he is on his way;
A lump is forming in your throat;
Can't keep the tears at bay.

Too soon the parting's over and done;
"How will he cope without me?"
You don't want to hear the answer;
You have to let him be.

For you must all the credit take;
You've taught them both to live;
Equipped with everything they need;
You've nothing left to give.

Your boys' success is down to you
And the mother's love they've known;
You've made them who they are today –
Respected men you've grown.

Only you can shed those tears
That a mother has inside;
But feel now, through this emptiness;
Your heart fill up with pride.

CHILDHOOD MEMORIES

The family would gather round,
The board would be prepared
And then the hunt to find the dice
That would rule how we all fared;
Sibling rivalries flourished then,
All striving to win the game;
Our favourite, snakes and ladders –
Being first was our only aim.

We'd all set off around the board
With only one thought in mind –
To win the game was everything,
And not be left behind;
Each of us cheering the others on,
All hoping that they would fail;
That fate would throw some cruel twist
And leave them at the tail.

So on the game would go and then –
Approaching the Finish Line,
But no! The dreadful tears that flowed,
You've landed on 99!
The biggest snake on the board was there
And down you'd fall to find
That you're the one who now is left
So many squares behind.

But losing is part of the game you see,
For those who finish first
Couldn't really do so,
Without those who fared the worst.

CHILD'S PLAY

I have had such a tiring day –
The things I've seen and done
Have left me here exhausted
But it was so much fun.

I've seen how children used to live
More than a hundred years ago;
I've ridden on a steam train too
And really enjoyed it so;

I've bounced all over a castle
That really was a joy –
I showed a little girl can have
As much fun as a boy.

I've ridden on a dinosaur
And driven a tractor too;
I saw a tram go rattling by
And waved as it drove through;

But now it's time to head for home
These memories I'll keep,
I'm locking all of them away
Before I fall asleep.

DÉJÀ VU

What on earth is happening?
I've seen all this before;
It's like a dream and yet it's real –
Don't like it any more.

I know it isn't happening,
The things around me are
Surreal and somewhat familiar,
They're taking me too far.

Yet if I know it isn't real
Why can't I stop this thing?
It just keeps going and going
It's making my head ring.

One scene after another
Even the people here
Are folk I've seen somewhere before –
This is something very queer.

My mind so slow to take it in;
It can't be real, yet it's so;
Everything that's round me now
Has passed, that's all I know.

And now it starts to fade away,
Life returns to what should be;
I shake my head to clear my thoughts;
My world's come back to me.

Can't pretend to understand it –
Simply a trick of the mind?
No matter how I search and search
The answer I'll never find.

DESPERATION

A 'basics' can of beans is all I can afford
Till my benefit comes through this week;
It won't be enough, I really know that Lord –
I need to find another thing with which to eek
This out for three long days or maybe more.

At home I have a couple of bits of bread I know
But I feel so down without the cash to spend
On simple foods to somehow keep me on the go;
I didn't ask for this, but can't see how to end
The mess I'm in – the lowest of the low.

Two years ago I lost my job, my wife walked out on me
But I was really ill back then, couldn't breathe, could hardly stand;
My world had turned itself on its head it seemed to be;
Now I'm living off the state, and holding out my hand
For food and drink to help me find my long-lost sanity.

They came and took my boys, gave them to someone new;
Said I wasn't fit to be a Dad and couldn't look after them;
The tears I shed watching as in the car they flew
To foster care, it broke my heart – I had no money then;
Oh Lord, I am so desperate, what is there I can do?

So think awhile, before you judge the lonely and in need –
We don't all choose this dreadful path to tread;
Sometimes it's just the way of things, so take heed,
Spare me a thought, and others too, before I end up dead
And my obituary is all that's left for you to read.

GOT TO WIN

Got to win, got to win –
It's so important to me;
I build a trap inside my head,
So subtle they cannot see.

Months it's taken to get here;
The unseen things I've done
To make sure that I'm successful;
I have to be the one.

The final scene is ready –
All angles covered to
Ensure her answer to me
Will last our whole lives through.

The tears fall free when I ask her
To forever be my wife;
Seconds delay seem like hours,
Her answer will rule my life.

'Oh yes' she finally whispers;
I have won the mental game,
I have won the heart of this angel
And now she bears my name.

HIGH AND DRY

The rush of water 'gainst polished hull
Is waiting now for me –
A few more yards until I dip
My keel into the sea;
And then it's off around the world,
I'll sail the oceans deep,
I'll see the far-off lands again
I remember in my sleep.

And everyone will stop to stare
As I go racing by –
My sails all billowed in the wind,
Pointing to the sky;
My sleek blue sides awash with spray
As bow dips down again;
Then sails all furled as I draw near
My latest journey's end.

MY STORM-TOSSED LIFE

I am but a poor little fluttering bird,
Blown hither and thither in fickle gale;
Drenched my feathers
And battered my frame;
Squirming I fly to nest
Of brittle twigs and moss.

MY LIFELINE

I rouse from slumber, it's another day
Of struggling somehow through this living hell;
This frame of mine is now an empty shell
Until my lifeline soon does call my way –
No other human watches this decay
And share with me my prison, this damned cell!
To think! I used to be so fit, so well;
There's only one to help me where I lay –
My carer out of love and sacrifice
Will wash and dress me, feed me breakfast too;
His promise made till life is finally through,
Does everything he deems will here suffice.
My boy, my son, this was not meant to be –
To be a lifeline, caring just for me.

OH WHAT A DAY!

Oh what a day, a lucky day,
One that my dreams have seen;
'Tis magic that it came my way
(Could otherwise have been).
Up with the lark the morn to greet
And all the travails I must meet –
Up with the lark
Up with the lark
My racing heart just missed a beat.

Oh what a day, a lucky day,
A song is in my heart.
I've practised all the things to say
For me to play my part.
The sun beats down upon the scene;
Spreads out its warmth and rays serene –
The sun beats down
The sun beats down
My spirit is so very keen.

Oh what a day, a lucky day,
She's coming now for me.
I hope that all I've wished for may
Let the blessèd world see
Such wedded bliss is to be mine
We'll start our life with arms entwined –
Such wedded bliss
Such wedded bliss
Is a thing that's truly divine.

QUESTION OF POWER

Who's the most powerful on this Earth?
There are candidates galore –
The United States would have us believe
It is them, but then there's more.

Others would protest at such a thought;
The Russians or even Chinese?
Japan is strong and Europe as well
But there's someone stronger than these.

Yes, they are all very powerful,
Each in their own different way;
But as for it being a nation?
It's none of these I say.

Strong as we humans consider ourselves,
There's nothing (we have) to master
The weather, the seas, the wind's ability
To wreak havoc by way of 'disaster'.

Mother Nature's armoury has weapons
Beyond our wildest dreams –
Storms that can destroy a country;
We're power-*less* it seems.

You don't have to be strong to be powerful
There's another side to see;
A gentler and amazing side
Shows what power can really be

For then we stand in wonderment
At the things that She can do;
Creating pictures so colourful
In shades of every hue.

Each and every morning She's there
Somewhere in this World,
Blazing colour across the skies
As another dawn's unfurled.

But we see power as strength and might
And strive to be 'the best';
Yet all our power is made by man,
'Twould never stand the test.

How could humans generate a force
To bring mountains to their knees?
Demolish towns and villages?
Create those mountainous seas?

Earthquakes, storms and howling winds
More powerful than anything
That any nation on this Earth
With all its might can bring!

Volcanoes, heat waves, freezing cold,
Fire and flood and more;
We have no power to conquer them –
They shake us to our core.

So why must we attempt to be
Stronger than one another
And wreck the Earth in doing so
To be above our brother?

We all send aid to 'disaster zones'
No matter where or who;
But why only in adversity
Must we the right thing do?

Isn't Mother Nature telling us
To help our fellow man?
To share resources and our time
And be the best we can?

Think of the times She's pulled a stunt –
We've always pulled together;
Why can't we do it all the time
And be like this for ever?

Oh yes, we have our powerful things,
But nothing can compare
With Mother Nature's awesome strength;
And She'll always be there.

SONNET TO LIFE

I think of death and what it means to me;
A challenge 'tis that puts thoughts to the test;
Yet we shall each within this darkness rest
Someday, in truth it's where we all will be.
How will it come? I do not truly see,
For blind am I to know which way is best
When heart stops beating deep within my breast –
I pray that I will let it set me free
From all the travails of my weary life,
(Whose days are numbered and so very few)
To take me to a place I never knew;
Away from all this misery and strife
But Death stalks not near me, of that I'm sure –
Relief! I shed all thoughts of death once more.

THANK YOU

T ill the desert sands are frozen and
H ell has done the same
A lways there beside me
N ever finding blame
K indness, time and love you give
Y our heart beats just for me
O n and on for evermore
U ntil eternity

THE DAY IS DONE

The hard day's work is over now
And hay is gathered in
So I have just been cast aside –
Punished for my sin.

My crime? I failed to bale, you see
The way I'm meant to do
Meant extra work for farmer's lads
Who kicked and cursed me too.

No doubt I'll lie here many years
Midst grasses tall and green
And soon no-one will know I'm here
For I will not be seen

And how I pine for the glory days
Of baling, weeks on end
From farm to farm, they used me well
But I'll not work again.

So cast a thought for us broken souls
Whose working day is o'er
As newer more robust machines
Mean we'll work nevermore.

THE BELFRY BELL

Off the Main Street in East Calder
Lies a church in ruins now –
It's not been used for centuries
It's had its final bow.

St Cuthbert's Church has seen some life
Since Eleven-forty-eight;
It passed through many changes too,
Before its final fate.

A place of worship for the folk
Of the Calders and surrounds;
Those that took their final trip
Are in its confines found.

Five hundred years it kept its watch
O'er the village's west end –
But upkeep wasn't good back then
And the roof began to bend.

Despite requests that help be sent
To keep a church to fill,
A new one was to take its place
In Kirknewton, up the hill.

And so, mid-18th century,
St Cuthbert's closed its door –
The time had come to leave it there,
Cross the threshold nevermore.

Go have a look at what is there
Remaining on this site –
The belfry's just an empty space
Where jackdaws rest from flight.

Still standing in the churchyard
But only just, you see
The gable ends are leaning out
The windows blocked with scree

The door is sealed over now
And the wind is all that fills
The body of this empty kirk
Then escapes across its sills.

But there are tombs of 'landed' folk
Like the Hares of Calder Hall
The Wilkies of Ormiston House lie here
Beneath the silent belfry tall

No bell it has, so silent stands –
A sign of days gone by;
We'll never hear the chimes again
From the bell swinging on high.

And now this reminder of our past
Seems slumped and somewhat worn;
With its weather-beaten stonework
Looks sad and so forlorn.

The blinded windows no longer see
The door never opens wide;
The people of East Calder
Will never step inside.

The bell has gone forever
And plants take root within
The open floors and crevices –
It really is a sin.

WHY?

I'm nailed to this tree
And think what might have been
This world, not ready, has punished me
They cannot see what I have seen

But Lord, dear Father, you must know
Your way could come to be
Why not Father? I could succeed
So why hast thou forsaken me?

SAUL

Saul was a non-believer
Who, with the Romans, sought
To remind these new Christ followers
They were doing not what they ought

He was a Pharisee from Tarsus
Learned in the ancient ways
Of the elders who had taught them
With the words of bygone days

He was there at Stephen's stoning
May well have thrown a stone
With his hatred of Christ's disciples
He did not stand alone

They persecuted the Church back then
Took prisoners as well
To follow in Christ's footsteps
Must have been a living Hell

But one day Saul went to Damascus
More Christ followers to find
And bring them back to Jerusalem
He was suddenly struck blind!

A blazing light surrounded him
And all his men could hear
Jesus' voice was asking him
Why disciples lived in fear

"Why do you persecute me Saul?"
Saul himself was so afraid
He saw the Lord in front of him
Jesus' masterstroke was played

It wasn't just a vision though
Jesus stood there by the road
Told him to go down to the town
Lay down his heavy load.

Saul saw the error of his ways
Became a follower devout
Preached Jesus is the Son of God
Of this there is no doubt

He changed his name to Paul and then
Wandered throughout the land
Helping start Christianity
Achieve the upper hand.

THAT MAN SHALL LIVE

Imagine the scene – long, long ago
And the fear there must have been
In the hearts of those poor shepherds,
Not believing what they had seen.

The brightest light shone in the sky
And in its midst a sound –
So soft and gentle, calling them
Way down there, on the ground.

Don't be afraid, it seemed to say,
The sound falling through the air;
Such glorious words and music clear,
Such beauty beyond compare.

For this is the love we can't possess –
Can only try to understand
That someone special came to us
That night, in the form of man.

This is the love of a father
For everyone here on earth;
To send to us his only son
And announce his humble birth.

Thousands of years have ticked slowly by
And yet we all remember
To celebrate this special birth
Each and every December.

So, give your gifts to all you love
But remember in your strife –
Jesus isn't just for Christmas –
Jesus is for Life!

THOMAS'S PRAYER

Where are you now Lord Jesus,
Who came from Heaven above?
Who guided us and taught us
To live in the shadow of love

They said you'd come to free us
From the troubles that we bear
And deliver us from evil
By showing how much you care

You came into this city
Hailed as '**Saviour of All**'
And then within a few days
We witnessed your dramatic fall

They put you on trial, Jesus,
Accused you of blasphemous crimes
They said you claimed to be King
Of the Jews in these troubled times

They stripped you of your clothing
And beat you so brutally;
Then garbed you in royal robes
And nailed you to this tree.

Where are you now Lord Jesus
After your entry here?
How you carried your burden
Knowing that death was so near.

You hang there bruised and battered,
So how can you help us now?
How do we go on without you?
Lord Jesus, please tell us how.

Those words you said, "It is finished!"
Does it really mean us too?
Why do you choose to leave us?
Oh Lord, what are we to do?

Where are you now Lord Jesus,
Now, when we need you most?
You hang there, dead on a tree
And our redemption is lost

A WORD IN YER LUG, DEAR RABBIE

May Ah hae a word yer bardship?
Jist a wee bit o' advice
Ah've heard that ye've been ganging aboot
A wick dippin', aince or twice

Oh Rabbie, 'tis yersel' ye ken
Should hang yer heid in shame
Fer while ye're oot wi' a' yer pals
Yer wee wife's left at hame

Wee Jeanie hasnae the life o' a dug
Looking efter a' they wains
D'ye nae think on her noo an' then
Amidst yer romantic refrains

Or is it, in yer e'en at least
A game fer ye tae play
Fer a man's a man fer a' that
Is that whit yer thochts say?

Whit maitters it ye've a bonnie wife
While maidens seek ye oot?
Ah'll tell ye this ye muckle de'il
Yer soul's as black as soot!

Ye hae an eye fer the lassies true
An' mony o' thaim fer thee
Jist waitin' fer a chance tae hae
A fling wi' a celebrity

Ye've writ aboot a' kind o' things
Fae lice tae a hert's desire
But 'tisnae ae fond kiss ye need
Tae quench yer rampant fire

Ye maun tak' yer leave o' womenfolk
Ye've a wife whae sits at hame
Hearing a' these marv'lous wurds
Ye speer tae anither ain

'tis sure tae mak ye weak ma lad
Ye'll no' see thirty eight
Afore the Laird comes callin' ye
By then 'twill be too late

So Rabbie, please ging back again
Tae Jeanie, sweet an' fair
An' speer yer magic lyrics, aye
She does deserve her share

Fer she hae nursed yer mony wains
And herd the tales ye tell
Ne'er thinkin' o' the hert ye broke
Nor o' the tears that fell

Puir Jeanie's gi'ed ye everythin'
Ony man could e'er hae needed
She disnae want tae hear nae mair
O' the lassies that ye've seeded

She kep' it a' inside her heid
No' mony weemin wuid
Ye've a' the luck o' the de'il hi'sel'
A wife tae dae as ye bid.

So tak ma advice an' ging back hame
Tae the red, red rose whae bides
An' beg forgiveness o' Jeanie brave
Whae's lo'ed ye since she was yer bride

58